The
WORD
EFFECT
Study Guide

The
WORD
EFFECT
Study Guide

7 Simple Words to
Create Your Most Beautiful Life

by

BECKY JANE KEMP
www.becomingwithbecky.com

LEADERSHIP
BOOKS

To order this title, or for more information on Becoming with Becky, please call

801-205-5797

Published by Leadership Books, Inc. Las Vegas, NV – New York, NY
LeadershipBooks.com

ISBN: 9781965401392 (Paperback)

To those ready to embrace the extraordinary power of words and make lasting changes in their lives, this study guide is dedicated to YOU!

Even though life often surprises us with moments where we find ourselves saying, "This is not the plan," may you discover, through the power of words, how to shift from obstacles to solutions.

A heartfelt thank you to God, for placing this truth in my heart, and to my husband, Kris, and my five amazing boys, for being the constant encouragement that empowers me to become my best self.

This guide is my hope for you to take each word as a small, actionable step toward joyful living. As you work through this study guide, remember to embrace the HOW—honesty, open-mindedness, and willingness.

May each lesson encourage you to take one simple word and create your most beautiful life.

CONTENTS

How to Get the Most Out of this Study Guide 5

Helpful Tips 7

Intro 8

Chapter 1: BECOMING AWARE OF YOUR WORDS 15

Chapter 2: ACKNOWLEDGE 25

Chapter 3: ASK 29

Chapter 4: ACCEPT 33

Chapter 5: ABUNDANCE 37

Chapter 6: ACTION 41

Chapter 7: APPRECIATE 45

Chapter 8: ASPIRE 49

Conclusion: The Word Effect's Never -Ending Cycle of Joyful Living 53

HOW TO GET THE MOST OUT OF THIS STUDY GUIDE

This study guide was created for those who feel ready to move beyond the uncertainty, fear, and doubt that can cloud everyday life. By choosing your words intentionally, you will harness the power of focus to unlock your potential, inspire authentic leadership, and amplify creativity. It's a journey of discovering who you truly are, with words serving as your compass.

Designed to work alongside *The Word Effect* book and video course, this guide presents the very steps I focused on—and continue to use—to create my most beautiful life. Each chapter introduces a power word that will guide you to reflect, reframe, and refocus your perspective. While life's circumstances may not change, your choice of words can lead you to experience greater joy and purpose.

As you read, *always remember*: "Your focus determines your reality." Use this guide as a resource to come back to, especially during life's challenges, and let these words open new possibilities. With honesty, open-mindedness, and willingness, you'll see these small, consistent shifts bring out the change you desire.

Now, step forward, ready to discover the life you're meant to live. Set an intention to truly engage with each word, reflect on your journey, and apply these words daily as you move from the sidelines into the most extraordinary version of your life. This has been my experience, and I share it knowing it can be yours as well.

With Joy,

Becky

Individual Study: Begin each session with a moment of prayer or quiet reflection, inviting honesty, open-mindedness, and willingness as you move through the material. This openness is the foundation for real change, allowing you to see the power of words in action.

This study guide works best with *The Word Effect* book or video course. I recommend reading or watching the course first, then using the guide chapter by chapter to build on each word. Each word in the guide builds on the last, leading you through a layered journey that supports lasting transformation.

As you work, use a notebook to write down your thoughts, responses, and any phrases or words that resonate with you. Writing things down helps reinforce what you're learning, allowing these concepts to become second nature over time. I love writing down simple reminders or power phrases—these words become touchstones that keep my focus and direction upward, even when life pulls me in other directions.

Also, remember the importance of T.R.Y.—Today, Redirect Your thoughts for good. Change often starts in the small, consistent steps, so stay patient and trust the process. End each session with a moment of gratitude or prayer to ground what you've gained.

Group Study: For group study, follow the same tips with added steps to support a meaningful and safe environment. Begin and end with group prayer or reflection, inviting everyone to approach the discussion with honesty, open-mindedness, and willingness to listen. Encourage participants to come prepared, having read the chapter or watched the video, so that each person brings their own insights.

Emphasize confidentiality to foster a safe space, where everyone feels free to share. Writing is just as powerful in groups—encourage each member to write down any power phrases or words that speak to them. Practicing T.R.Y. together can strengthen everyone's growth, as each person's unique experiences offer fresh perspectives. Group study provides the additional strength of connection, enriching each person's understanding of the Word Effect.

INTRO

To begin your journey through The Word Effect: 7 Simple Words to Create Your Most Beautiful Life, start by watching the introductory video of The Word Effect course or reading the introduction in the book, titled "The Extraordinary Power of Words." In this chapter, we'll uncover how words act as a compass, guiding your thoughts, actions, and ultimately, your life's direction. Reflect on how words currently shape your life and the possibilities that lie ahead by intentionally choosing empowering words. Remember to jot down your insights—capturing your thoughts in writing helps you make these powerful ideas a part of your daily life.

SUMMARY:

In this introduction, we explore the transformative power of words and their profound ability to shape our thoughts, actions, and ultimately, our reality. Rather than focusing solely on our circumstances, The Word Effect encourages us to recognize the impact of our interpretations and the stories we tell ourselves. This concept empowers you to awaken your story and create the life you've always envisioned. By intentionally choosing words that lead you toward joy and purpose, you can guide your mind with clarity and direction, opening doors to creativity and innovation.

Words are the building blocks of our personal narratives, influencing how we perceive ourselves and the world around us. With an understanding of intentional language, you can actively craft your story, face challenges with resilience, and shift from a place of negativity to one of joy and optimism. The introduction emphasizes that your highest potential lies within your power to choose words that unlock it—making each day an opportunity to create and live your most beautiful life.

QUESTIONS FOR REFLECTIONS:

1. **The Power of a Single Word**

   Reflecting on how a single word can shape our emotions or actions, I think back to a moment that taught me just how powerful words can be. In 2005, I had my heart set on hearing one word at a doctor's appointment: "girl." With three sons already,

I had dreamed about adding a daughter to our family. When the doctor instead announced, "boy," my heart sank, and the words *"this is not the plan"* filled my mind. My husband, however, was overjoyed; he took the same word—*"boy"—*as exciting news.

In that moment, I realized that words hold no inherent meaning until we attach our own. While my husband saw *"boy"* as part of our beautiful unfolding life, I viewed it as a deviation from my hopes. Recognizing that it was my thoughts, not the word itself, that created my emotions helped me shift my perspective and experience more joy and gratitude.

Think of a time when a single word had a profound impact on you. Was it a word of encouragement, a label, or even a simple response that shifted your mindset or behavior? Write down your experience and reflect on how that word influenced you. What did you learn about yourself, and how might you reshape your response to words in the future?

2. **Circumstances vs. Thoughts**

In *The Word Effect: 7 Simple Words to Create Your Most Beautiful Life*, I explore how our circumstances don't determine our happiness or fulfillment—it's our thoughts that do. Five years after having my fourth son, life surprised me with another boy. Becoming a mother to five sons was a blessing, though not one I had planned for. Initially, I felt overwhelmed, thinking, *"This isn't the plan!"* My thoughts filled with feelings of inadequacy and frustration, not because of the circumstances themselves, but because of the words I was choosing to put on each day.

These situations taught me that while I couldn't control my circumstances, I could control my response to them. By shifting my focus with intentional words, I began to replace feelings of *"overwhelmed"* and *"not enough"* with thoughts that empowered me and brought me joy.

Reflect on your own challenging situations. How do you typically respond? Are there patterns in your thoughts that tend to arise? Take a moment to identify any recurring themes and consider how changing the words you focus on could reshape your experience. What words could guide you toward feelings of peace or empowerment?

3. **Choosing Words to Start the Day**

Imagine waking up each day with a conscious choice of the words you want to embody. We've all had those mornings where the first five minutes are blissful... until we get out of bed! It's a reminder that we have control over our focus and mindset, no matter what.

Consider choosing words or phrases to "put on" that set the tone for your day. Words like "*grateful,*" "*calm,*" or "*embrace your greatness*" can shift your attitude and actions in powerful ways, helping you recognize your strengths even amid chaos or setbacks.

What positive words or affirmations could you choose to shape your day and mindset? How might shifting your language or internal dialogue influence your ability to move forward? Start with one or two words each morning and watch how this simple habit transforms your experience.

4. **Breaking Through Feeling Stuck**

Think about a recent experience where you felt completely stuck or overwhelmed. For me, one of these moments was deciding to write *The Word Effect*. The thought of writing a book felt too big, too daunting, and I was flooded with self-doubt. I kept thinking, "*This is just too much—I'll never finish,*" which only amplified my feelings of being overwhelmed.

But as I shifted my internal dialogue from "*I can't*" to "*I'll take it one step at a time*" and focused on words like "*progress,*" "*learn,*" and "*create,*" something changed. Each word helped me embrace the journey instead of getting lost in the outcome.

Think back to a time when you felt similarly. How might shifting your language or internal dialogue in that situation have influenced your ability to move forward? Write down words that might have helped and consider how they could have opened a new path. This exercise is a reminder that our words are indeed our compass, guiding us forward one step at a time.

5. **Separating Fact from Story**

In *The Word Effect*, I once shared a belief I used to hold: "*Good things happen to good people, and bad things happen to bad people.*" But that's just a story. Life doesn't always go as planned, and it isn't necessarily a reflection of our choices—it's simply life on life's terms.

Consider how you might separate facts from the stories you tell yourself. Often, these stories keep us feeling stuck. Have you ever told yourself a story like this?

Identify one narrative you currently hold about yourself or your life. Does it lead you toward the results you want, or does it hold you back? Are your stories really true, or are they just that—stories? Take a few minutes to identify one story, separate it from the facts, and then rewrite it in a way that focuses on truth and allows you to move forward with a clearer, more empowering perspective

WORD POWER ACTIVITY:

Reflecting on your words and the energy they carry is a powerful step in creating the life you desire. Let's start with a few reflections and practical actions to put this into practice.

1. **Daily Vocabulary Check-In**

   Take a moment to think about the words you habitually use or "put on" each day. Reflect on any words or phrases you find yourself using repeatedly—whether they're positive, neutral, or even discouraging. Write them here.

2. **Aligning Words with Your Vision**

   Next, reflect on the mindset and outcomes you desire in life. Write down the qualities, aspirations, or goals you're working toward. What words do you want to embrace that will guide you in that direction? This practice helps anchor your intentions in a clear vision.

Each morning, I like to ask myself, "What words do I choose to put on today?" It's a simple reminder that I'm in charge of my focus and can shape my day with intentional language.

3. **Choose Your Word or Affirmation**

   Here's my challenge to you: choose one empowering word or affirmation for today—something that truly resonates with your aspirations and embodies the mindset you want to cultivate. Here are some examples to inspire you:

- » **I am enough.**
- » **Embrace your greatness.**
- » **I trust the process.**
- » **Today, I choose joy.**
- » **I have everything I need to succeed.**
- » **I am capable and courageous.**
- » **Abundance flows to me with ease.**
- » **I am exactly where I am meant to be.**
- » **I choose gratitude over worry.**
- » **I focus on progress, not perfection.**

Write your chosen word or affirmation here:

Then, keep it visible throughout your day—on an index card, a sticky note, or as a reminder on your phone.

4. **Reflect and Journal**

At the end of the day, take a few minutes to journal about your experience. Reflect on how focusing on this word or affirmation influenced your mindset, actions, and overall outlook. Did it shift your perspective? How did it shape your day?

This practice takes time and consistency, so try it for several weeks. With intentional repetition, you'll begin to see how incorporating empowering language can shape your daily experiences, guiding you closer to your most beautiful life.

JOURNAL PAGE

CHAPTER 1:

To start Chapter 1, Becoming Aware of Your Words, begin by watching the first video in *The Word Effect* course or reading the introduction in *The Word Effect: 7 Simple Words to Create Your Most Beautiful Life*. In this chapter, we'll explore the importance of recognizing the words we use daily and how they silently shape our thoughts, actions, and perceptions. Words are more than just expressions—they are powerful tools that direct our lives, much like a compass. By becoming aware of the words you "put on," you can begin to shift your mindset and open up new possibilities for joy, success, and self-discovery.

Take the time to reflect on the words that have been influencing your thoughts and jot down your discoveries. Writing helps reinforce these ideas and supports your journey toward creating the life you desire.

BECOMING AWARE OF YOUR WORDS

Your Words Matter—Discover Your Word Effect

"You can spend the time distressed, discontent, distracted, discouraged, dissatisfied or you can spend the time enjoying engaging, enriched. The only decision you have to make today is what you do with your time."
—Ann Voskamp

SUMMARY:

To begin your journey with *The Word Effect: 7 Simple Words to Create Your Most Beautiful Life*, start by watching the first video in *The Word Effect* course or reading Chapter 1 in the book, *Becoming Aware of Your Words*. In this chapter, I share how I found myself stuck in a cycle of dissatisfaction and discontent. Despite all the good things in my life, I wasn't truly happy. My thoughts were constantly filled with "if only" statements—if only certain things would change, then I'd be content. But these "if only" thoughts kept me distracted, anxious, and overwhelmed with negative self-talk.

As I opened up to my husband about these feelings, I saw how our perspectives differed. Where he saw optimism, I saw discouragement. He even pointed out that I never seemed happy, which was hard to hear but true. That moment was pivotal for me. I became aware of the words filling my mind—*distraction*, *despair*, and *discontent*—and realized that they were shaping my reality.

I cried out to God in frustration, and I felt the answer come: "Change your words." Those words marked the beginning of my journey. By changing the words I focused on, I could change my experience of life itself. I invite you to reflect on the words you currently "put on" each day. Are they empowering you or keeping you stuck? Use this chapter to start noticing your thoughts and consider what it would mean to choose new words, ones that guide you toward peace, joy, and fulfillment. Write down your insights—recording them will help you make lasting changes as you move through this journey.

Reflection question #1:

Are you a negative thinker?

Reflection question #2:

How much of a habitual cycle of negative thinking is affecting your ability to create the kind of life you were meant to lead?

As you go through this workbook, take a moment to reflect: if you're here, it's likely that you, too, have experienced feelings of discontent and negativity. You might find yourself wondering why, despite all the good around you, it's hard to shake that dissatisfaction. Often, the source of these feelings is deeply connected to the words and thoughts we habitually focus on.

Negativity begets negativity. I've found that most of what we fear, avoid, or feel resentment toward isn't about the actual events in our lives but about the negative words we use to describe those events to ourselves. Our thoughts and words shape our feelings, and those feelings determine how we experience life. The way you talk to yourself and the words you choose have power—they create your reality.

As we move forward, keep this in mind. Becoming aware of the words you're putting on each day is a first step toward shifting from negativity to a mindset that can bring you true peace and joy. Take your time with each reflection, and let this workbook guide you in exploring how intentional words can reshape your experience.

The Power of Awareness: How Negative Thoughts Take Over

Did you know that the average person has between 16,000 and 60,000 thoughts daily? The National Science Foundation has shown that most of these thoughts occur subconsciously. What's even more surprising—and important to understand as you move through this study guide—is that about 80% of these thoughts are negative. Even more, 95% are the same thoughts we carried from the day before.

This shows how easy it is to fall into patterns of negativity that repeat day after day. This doesn't mean that we're powerless; it simply highlights how our brains are wired. But with intentional language, we can shift this pattern. To overcome these habits, it requires what I call *breakthrough thinking*—the conscious choice to focus on words and thoughts that help us grow and thrive rather than keep us stuck.

Each time you choose a positive word, even if it's just one word a day, you're creating new pathways for joy, growth, and resilience. This guide, along with *The Word Effect* book and video course, is designed to help you put on those empowering words that allow you to live a beautiful, purposeful life.

Use this awareness exercise to track the number of negative vs. positive reflections. Watch how each small choice to "put on" a word of hope, kindness, or encouragement begins to turn the tide and reshape your mindset.

Negative Words vs. Positive Words

Words shape our thoughts, and our thoughts influence our actions. Let's start by getting clear on which types of words you tend to use more often. On the left, list some words that carry a negative tone; on the right, list positive words that bring you strength and joy. Ask yourself: which side do I draw from more often?

Negative	Positive
Overwhelmed	Empowered
Discouraged	Hopeful
Stressed	Calm
Inadequate	Worthy
Doubtful	Confident
Fearful	Courageous

The Model for Shaping Outcomes

As a Life Coach, I use a simple yet powerful model to show how our words and thoughts lead to the outcomes we experience. Here's what it looks like:

Circumstance	Thoughts	Feelings	Actions	Results

Circumstances alone are neutral, but the thoughts we attach to them create our feelings. Those feelings then drive our actions, which ultimately shape our results. Use this model to track an experience this week, noting the thought that arose, the feeling it generated, the action you took, and the result it created.

Tracking Negativity Bias: Reflections for Growth

Studies show that criticism and negative experiences tend to stick with us more than compliments or positive moments. Negative words can be powerful, but the good news is that we have a choice in how we respond. Use the following worksheet to bring awareness to your natural responses:

Experience	Negative Reflection	Positive Reflection

At the end of each day, tally how often you leaned toward negative thoughts and how often you consciously chose positive ones. This awareness is a foundational step in shifting toward a life of intentional, empowering words.

Reflection question #3:

Think about the National Science Foundation's research findings regarding human thoughts per day. How does the prevalence of negative thoughts in your mind impact your daily experiences and interactions.?

Embracing Positivity: Rewiring Your Brain

In *The Word Effect* course and book, I shared a story about my son, Kayden, who discovered a powerful way to combat negativity by singing in the church choir. Through this experience, he "put on" words filled with hope, joy, and goodness, and it made a real difference in his outlook. When we intentionally choose positive words or activities, we begin to shift our internal focus and reduce the weight of negative thinking. Take a moment and ask yourself: *What can I incorporate into my life to combat negativity?*

Exercise: Write down three specific words or phrases that resonate with hope and joy. These could be from a favorite song, a quote, or even a personal affirmation. Reflect on how you could use these words in your day-to-day life to reshape your mindset.

"Emotional Childishness" and Breaking Free from Negativity

We often get stuck in patterns of negative thinking because of what I call *emotional childishness*—the tendency to avoid difficult emotions or blame external factors rather than taking personal responsibility. Emotional childishness can keep us in a loop of anxiety and negativity, which is especially true for perfectionists like myself. I had to learn how to train my brain, and it's an ongoing journey for many of us.

Our brains naturally gravitate toward three responses:

1. **Seek Pleasure**: Craving instant gratification or "feel-good" distractions.
2. **Avoid Pain**: Steering clear of difficult feelings or situations.
3. **Conserve Energy**: Choosing the easiest or most familiar path.

These tendencies are protective, but they can also keep us stuck in negativity if we let them dominate our mindset. Fixating on negativity is one way the brain tries to protect us from perceived danger. Recognizing this pattern is the first step to overcoming it.

Exercise: Building Your Personal Positivity Practice

To help shift away from negativity bias, try this exercise:

1. **Identify** a situation where you felt negative or overwhelmed.
2. **Note** the immediate thoughts and emotions that arose. Were they focused on avoiding pain or staying comfortable?
3. **Rewrite** your response. How can you reframe this experience by choosing empowering words or actions that support growth?

By understanding these patterns and practicing intentional language, we create space for positive, courageous thinking that moves us forward.

Breaking Free from Negative Bias: The Pig in the Mud Analogy

Imagine a pig stuck in the mud. The pig might look around and realize it's not in the best place, maybe noticing other animals moving freely or seeing clearer fields up ahead. To get unstuck, it has to muster up the energy to pick itself up, confronting the discomfort of leaving its "comfortable" muddy spot. At first, the mud seems cozy and familiar, even though it's holding the pig back. Taking that first step out, however, can feel challenging—each movement forward brings new feelings and uncertainties. Does the pig continue, or does it decide that lying back down in the mud is easier?

This story of the pig in the mud is a powerful analogy for any area of our lives where we feel stuck. Sometimes we choose to stay in our "mud"—our familiar negative thoughts, habits, or comfort zones—because the idea of change feels too uncomfortable or difficult. Yet, staying there means sacrificing the potential of reaching a better place.

In *The Word Effect* book and video course, we talk about breaking free of this negative bias by taking responsibility for both our pain and our joy. This means recognizing that:

1. Happiness comes from within—stop expecting others to "make" you happy.
2. Security is an inner strength—stop relying on others to "make" you feel secure.
3. Only you have the power to change your feelings and break free from fear or anxiety.

When we sit in the "mud" of negative thoughts, it's our own language and perspective that keeps us there. Each word we choose affects the emotions we feel, which in turn influences the actions we take. Consider a part of your life where you might feel stuck. How could changing the words you use to describe it help you break free from limitations? Embrace that shift and take the first courageous step forward—one thought, one word, one choice at a time.

Word Power Activity

In *The Word Effect: 7 Simple Words to Create Your Most Beautiful Life*, I share the idea of becoming the "CEO" of your emotions and the "watcher" of your thoughts—a powerful concept that encourages you to take control of your inner dialogue and, in turn, shape your reality. When you take charge as CEO, you're deciding which thoughts to focus on, which to release, and which words will guide your day. This level of intentionality allows you to shift from a reactive mindset to one of empowered, purposeful thinking.

Reflect on this: as the CEO of your emotions, you're not at the mercy of your thoughts; rather, you're actively selecting words that support the life you want to create. You're leading your mind with clarity, not letting circumstances dictate how you feel, but instead choosing words that align with your purpose and goals. Being the "watcher" of your thoughts allows you to see patterns, challenge old beliefs, and replace negativity with words that uplift and inspire you to move forward.

Ask yourself: *How can I take more responsibility for my emotional well-being? How can I intentionally select words that support the life I aspire to create?* Consider a few empowering words or phrases that resonate with your vision and commit to incorporating these into your daily mindset.

By becoming the CEO of your emotions and the watcher of your thoughts, you're taking essential steps to "speak your success" and become an intentional leader of your mind. Take a moment now to write down some words or affirmations that will support you in becoming your best self and remember to "put on" these words each day, keeping your focus on success and fulfillment.

WORD POWER ACTIVITY:

Observe and write down your internal dialogue and the words you use to describe yourself, others, and your experiences.

_____

_____

_____

Did you notice any patterns of negative language or self-talk?

_____

_____

_____

Choose one area where you'd like to make a conscious shift in your language—for example, replacing self-criticism with self-compassion or reframing challenges as opportunity for growth.

_____

_____

_____

Throughout the day, practice using empowering words and affirmations in this area. Write down the words you will use here.

_____

_____

_____

How did this intentional language shift impacted your mindset, emotions, and interactions with others?

_____

_____

_____

CHAPTER 2:

To begin your journey through Chapter 2, *Acknowledge: The First Step to Becoming Your Authentic and Most Beautiful Life*, read this chapter in *The Word Effect: 7 Simple Words to Create Your Most Beautiful Life* or watch the corresponding segment in *The Word Effect* video course. In this chapter, we'll explore the transformative power of acknowledging your dreams, strengths, and even your challenges as a foundation for authentic living.

Take this opportunity to reflect on your current self-perception and the words you use to define it. Acknowledging where you are today is essential to understanding where you want to go. As you read, note any insights that arise—writing these down will help reinforce your commitment to your personal growth. Let's dive into the practice of acknowledgment, embracing your journey and discovering the impact intentional language can have on your life.

ACKNOWLEDGE

The First Step of Becoming Your Authentic and Most Beautiful Life

"The first step on the path to positive change in acknowledging that change is necessary and possible. Open yourself to the possibility of seeing the world in a new way. What do you have to lose?"
—Alex Blackwell

SUMMARY:

Welcome to Chapter 2, "Acknowledge"—the first step in your intentional journey of becoming the leader of your own life. In *The Word Effect: 7 Simple Words to Create Your*

Most Beautiful Life, we explore how to cultivate a mindset of acknowledgment by focusing on the language you use, such as the powerful difference between "I can" and "I can't" or the transformative effect of "I am" statements. This chapter invites you to intentionally recognize your dreams, desires, and potential, setting the foundation for a life led with courage and authenticity.

By practicing acknowledgment, you begin to cultivate a purposeful mindset that values growth and self-discovery over perfectionism. Through guided reflection, you'll challenge limiting beliefs, embrace vulnerability, and replace self-doubt with self-belief. Acknowledging your strengths, weaknesses, dreams, and desires opens the door to intentional leadership—a leadership that originates from within and guides you toward your most beautiful life.

As you read, focus on cultivating courage and authenticity in yourself by choosing empowering words. This is your invitation to engage fully with the possibilities that acknowledgment can create. Write down your insights, embrace each "I can," and begin to reframe your self-talk with words that uplift and inspire. By the end of this chapter, you'll have a clearer sense of how acknowledgment can be a catalyst for genuine, lasting change.

QUESTIONS FOR REFLECTION

1. **How do your daily thoughts shape your beliefs and actions?** Reflect on the role of intentional language in influencing how you see yourself and the world around you. Remember, each word you choose to put on either uplifts or holds you back.

2. **When have perfectionism or people-pleasing held you back?** Consider moments when these tendencies have limited your potential. How might intentionally acknowledging these patterns empower you to break free and live with more authenticity?

3. **How does acknowledging your current reality open doors for positive change?** Explore the connection between acknowledgment, self-acceptance, and intentional leadership. Remember that transformation begins with seeing things as they are.

4. **What role does vulnerability play in acknowledging your strengths and weaknesses?** Reflect on how intentional acknowledgment of both your strengths and areas for growth can lead to deeper authenticity and personal growth. How does vulnerability empower you in this journey?

5. **Is there a specific dream or ambition you've hesitated to acknowledge?** Identify one and think about how intentional acknowledgment can give you the courage to take a step forward. What is one small, meaningful action you can take today to begin pursuing this dream?

As you reflect on these questions, let acknowledgment be your guide. Embracing your true self and intentionally choosing words that empower you will lead you toward a life filled with courage, growth, and authenticity.

WORD POWER ACTIVITY

Challenge your fears by intentionally acknowledging your true potential. Start by writing down one thing you've been hesitant to acknowledge—whether it's a perceived weakness, a hidden desire, or an ambition close to your heart. Reflect on how bringing this truth to light empowers you to live with greater authenticity and courage.

Share your acknowledgment with someone you trust, and affirm your self-acceptance by writing, "I accept myself unconditionally, right now." Place this affirmation somewhere visible as a daily reminder of your intentional commitment to growth, courage, and authenticity.

CHAPTER 3:

As you begin Chapter 3, Ask: *The Power Word That Inspires Curiosity and Invites Change*, in *The Word Effect: 7 Simple Words to Create Your Most Beautiful Life,* or watch the corresponding video in *The Word Effect* course, immerse yourself in the transformative power of curiosity and intentional questioning. This chapter invites you to explore how asking thoughtful, purposeful questions can open doors, reveal new insights, and lead to meaningful changes in your life.

Throughout this chapter, reflect on how asking questions can shift your perspective and help you uncover new possibilities within yourself and your surroundings. Keep a journal close by to jot down any thoughts or revelations as they arise—writing reinforces clarity and turns ideas into actions. Allow this chapter to inspire you to ask with intention, embrace curiosity, and discover the potential for growth that lies within each question you choose to ask.

ASK

The Power Word That Inspires Curiosity and Invites Change

> "He who is afraid of asking is ashamed of learning."
> —Danish Proverb

SUMMARY:

Step into the transformative world of curiosity and change with the power word, *Ask.* In this chapter, we explore how curiosity, paired with intentional questioning, becomes a powerful tool for growth and discovery. Asking opens doors—it's the path to challenging your assumptions, stepping into vulnerability, and embracing a mindset of continuous learning. When we dare to ask, we initiate a journey of self-inquiry that allows us to tap into new possibilities and expand our lives in meaningful ways.

Curiosity fuels success by inviting us to see beyond the familiar and explore the potential within and around us. Through the art of asking the right questions, we find ourselves uncovering answers that challenge limiting beliefs, empowering us to make bold changes in both personal and professional aspects of our lives. As you learn to "ask" with intention, you'll cultivate resilience, embrace growth, and discover the beauty of living with a curious mind.

Let *Ask* be your guide to greater empowerment, growth, and fulfillment.

QUESTIONS FOR REFLECTION:

1. **Reflect on a time when you found it difficult to accept a particular part of your life or yourself.** What emotions arose as you resisted that acceptance, and how did it impact your sense of well-being? Acceptance often feels like freedom—but getting there can bring up complex feelings. Take a moment to explore how moving through that resistance affected you emotionally and mentally.

2. **Consider the quote, "Comparison is the thief of joy."** How has comparing yourself to others added to feelings of dissatisfaction or even self-doubt? Most of us fall into the "compare and despair" trap, and it can steal our peace. How might practicing acceptance free you from the cycle of comparison and allow you to truly appreciate where you are without judgment?

3. **Reflect on the connection between acceptance and personal responsibility.** When we accept ourselves and our circumstances, we're often more empowered to take control of our lives. How does acknowledging your reality, as it is right now, open the door to growth and fulfillment? Acceptance isn't about giving up on change—it's about starting from a place of clarity and authenticity, which can be incredibly empowering.

4. **Explore the idea that circumstances are neutral, and it's our thoughts about them that shape our experiences.** How might practicing acceptance shift your perspective and help you see situations with more positivity and possibility? Think

about a recent challenge and reflect on how choosing acceptance could create a healthier, more balanced approach.

5. **Consider the role of discomfort in personal growth and development.** Embracing discomfort isn't easy, yet it's essential for true growth. How can practicing acceptance of uncomfortable experiences contribute to resilience and inner strength? Reflect on times when discomfort led to growth, and think about how leaning into acceptance can make you stronger.

Take time to ponder each one thoughtfully and write down your reflections to commit to personal growth and self-acceptance.

WORD POWER ACTIVITY:

Challenge yourself to tap into the power of curiosity by asking one thought-provoking question each day for the next week. Begin each question with *How*—a word that directs your brain toward solutions and possibilities rather than obstacles. Choose questions that relate to areas in your personal or professional life where you seek clarity, want to set goals, or explore new aspirations. Reflect on the insights you gain from these questions each day and observe how this simple shift contributes to your ongoing growth and transformation.

CHAPTER 4:

As you explore into Chapter 4, *Accept: The Key to Greater Growth and Personal Development* in *The Word Effect: 7 Simple Words to Create Your Most Beautiful Life*, or view the related video in *The Word Effect* course, focus on the power of acceptance to foster deeper resilience, contentment, and progress. This chapter is crafted to help you shift from living in "if only" to embracing "what is," showing how acceptance lays the foundation for authentic joy and growth.

These study guide materials are designed to guide your reflections and actions, encouraging you to embrace acceptance as a daily practice. Refer back to the book and video course as you move through each question and activity to anchor your insights and intentions, allowing you to put acceptance into action and continue creating your most beautiful life.

ACCEPT

The Key to Greater Growth and Personal Development

> "You must take personal responsibility. You cannot change the circumstances, the seasons, or the wind, but you can change yourself. That is something you have charge of."
> —Jim Rohn

SUMMARY:

In this chapter, we explore the profound power of the word "Accept" and how embracing acceptance can become a cornerstone of personal growth and development. Acceptance is a key that unlocks a pathway to inner peace and resilience, allowing us to embrace the reality of our lives, rather than living in the shadows of "if only" or "when this changes." Here, I invite you to consider what it would mean to let go of resistance and find balance, contentment, and even joy in the present moment, just as it is.

When we accept, we give ourselves permission to release the struggle against our circumstances and instead focus on what we can influence—our mindset and our choices. This chapter combines timeless wisdom with personal stories to reveal how this approach leads us closer to our true selves. It teaches us that by accepting ourselves and our lives, we align with our inner truth, making space for genuine happiness and fulfillment.

You'll discover that acceptance isn't passive; it's an active, intentional shift toward personal responsibility. By cultivating a mindset of acceptance, we unlock a freedom that empowers us to move forward, unburdened by unrealistic expectations or regrets. Acceptance is not a final destination; it's a powerful daily choice that leads to resilience, deeper personal insight, and a joyful life lived in alignment with our true selves.

QUESTIONS FOR REFLECTION:

1. **Reflect on a time when you struggled to accept a particular aspect of your life or yourself.** What emotions surfaced as you resisted that acceptance, and how did it affect your overall well-being? Acceptance often feels like a release—but getting there can bring up all kinds of feelings. Explore how moving through that resistance impacted your mental and emotional health.

2. **Consider the quote, "Comparison is the thief of joy."** How has the habit of comparing yourself to others contributed to feelings of dissatisfaction or even self-doubt? We've all been there, feeling we fall short by measuring our lives against others. Reflect on how practicing acceptance could free you from the cycle of "compare and despair" and allow you to embrace where you are, without judgment or pressure.

3. **Explore the connection between acceptance and personal responsibility.** When we accept ourselves and our circumstances, we often feel more empowered to take charge of our lives. How can acknowledging your present reality, as it is, open

the door to growth and fulfillment? Acceptance doesn't mean giving up on change; it means starting from a place of clarity and authenticity, which can be incredibly empowering.

4. **Reflect on the idea that circumstances are neutral—it's our thoughts about them that shape our experiences.** How might practicing acceptance shift your perspective, helping you to see situations with more positivity or possibility? Think about a recent challenging situation and how choosing acceptance could shift your outlook, making room for a healthier and more balanced approach.

5. **Consider the role of discomfort in personal growth and development.** Embracing discomfort can be challenging, yet it's often essential for true growth. How can practicing acceptance of uncomfortable experiences contribute to resilience and inner strength? Reflect on moments when discomfort led you to growth, and consider how leaning into this acceptance could strengthen your journey.

These questions invite you to dig deep, reflecting on the ways acceptance can reshape your life. Take time to consider each question thoughtfully, writing down your reflections to solidify your commitment to personal growth and self-acceptance.

WORD POWER ACTIVITY:

1. Embrace Acceptance with Daily Reflection: Set aside a few moments each day to simply acknowledge and accept your thoughts, emotions, and circumstances as they are, without judgment or resistance. Notice how this small act of acceptance influences your mindset and sense of well-being. Over time, you may find it becomes a comforting ritual that brings you more peace and clarity.

2. Shift from "If Only" to "What Is": Catch yourself when you start falling into the "If Only" trap—wishing things were different or longing for a past that could have been. In that moment, challenge yourself to shift your focus. Embrace the "What Is" mentality, letting go of regret or longing. Gently bring your attention back to the present and practice accepting things as they are. This shift can open you to new possibilities and ground you in the beauty of the present moment.

Remember, acceptance is a process—take it one day at a time.

CHAPTER 5:

To begin exploring Chapter 5, "Abundance," I invite you to read this chapter in *The Word Effect: 7 Simple Words to Create Your Most Beautiful Life* or watch the corresponding video in *The Word Effect* course. In this chapter, we dive into the profound impact of cultivating an abundance mindset, focusing on progress rather than perfection.

As you go through this chapter, consider how an abundance mindset can help you shift your attention away from what's lacking and focus on what is growing and expanding in your life. Jot down your reflections and observations—writing helps to make these insights more concrete and actionable. Let this chapter inspire you to embrace progress and recognize the blessings already present in your journey, transforming your focus from scarcity to abundance.

ABUNDANCE

The Power Word That Focuses Your Attention on Progress over Perfection

> "Abundance is not something we acquire. It is something
> we tune into."
> —Wayne Dyer

SUMMARY:

In Chapter 5, we dive into the transformative power of the word "Abundance" as the foundation for a life focused on progress over perfection. Through this guiding word, you're invited to shift from a mindset of scarcity to one of abundance, recognizing the wealth of blessings, opportunities, and potential already present in your life. Embracing an abundant perspective fosters a deeper sense of gratitude, contentment, and fulfillment, allowing you to celebrate progress without the weight of perfectionism.

Drawing on personal stories and uplifting insights, this chapter illuminates how an abundance mindset can profoundly impact your journey. By intentionally choosing words that reflect the abundance of goodness surrounding you, you'll discover a new sense of freedom and purpose. This approach frees you from the constant striving for "more" or "perfect" and empowers you to see each step forward as meaningful progress. As you cultivate this abundant mindset, you'll find yourself aligned with the life you truly want to create—a life full of richness, growth, and joy.

Choosing abundance as a core principle isn't just a mindset; it's a daily practice that gently shifts your focus from what's missing to what's possible. Let the power of abundance be your compass, guiding you toward your most beautiful life.

QUESTIONS FOR REFLECTION:

1. **Reflect on Scarcity vs. Abundance**. Think of a time when you felt stuck in a scarcity mindset, focusing on what you lacked rather than what you already had. How did this perspective shape your thoughts, emotions, and actions? How might embracing an abundance mindset shift this experience?

2. **Reflect on Scarcity vs. Abundance**. Think of a time when you felt stuck in a scarcity mindset, focusing on what you lacked rather than what you already had. How did this perspective shape your thoughts, emotions, and actions? How might embracing an abundance mindset shift this experience?

3. **Progress Over Perfection**. Consider the concept of a circular motion where progress is prioritized over perfection. How does focusing on progress allow you to overcome the paralysis of perfectionism and take meaningful steps toward your goals?

4. **Failure as a Growth Tool**. Reflect on the role of failure in the pursuit of success. How does accepting failure as a natural part of growth contribute to your personal and professional development? How might this shift in perspective free you from the fear of making mistakes?

5. **Rising Above the Crab Mentality.**The "crab mentality" describes the tendency to pull others down rather than lift each other up. How does this mindset affect individual and collective success? How can you focus on elevating both yourself and those around you?

6. **Practicing Abundance Daily**. What are some ways you can incorporate abundance into your daily life? How can you cultivate gratitude, celebrate progress, and intentionally choose words that reflect an abundant mindset?

WORD POWER ACTIVITY:

1. **Gratitude Journaling for Abundance**. Practice the art of gratitude journaling by taking a few moments each day to recognize the blessings that already surround you. Write down three things you're grateful for and consider how each one contributes to a deeper sense of abundance and well-being. Notice how this simple practice can shift your focus from what's missing to what's thriving in your life.

2. **Replace Scarcity with Abundance**. Challenge yourself to transform any negative self-talk or scarcity-based thinking into words of abundance and empowerment. Whenever you catch yourself focusing on lack or limitation, pause and intentionally choose words that affirm abundance, possibility, and growth. This conscious shift will help you embrace a mindset of fullness and opportunity.

By actively practicing these small steps, you'll begin to cultivate an abundant mindset that empowers you to create your most beautiful life.

CHAPTER 6:

To engage deeply with Chapter 6, "Action," I recommend diving into *The Word Effect: 7 Simple Words to Create Your Most Beautiful Life* or watching this chapter's video in *The Word Effect* course. Here, we explore the essential power of taking intentional action as the energy that propels you forward on the path to joyful living.

Taking action, however small, can be the spark that transforms intentions into progress. This chapter encourages you to examine how purposeful steps, fueled by a commitment to your goals, create momentum and open doors to new possibilities. Reflect on your current actions and consider how to align them with the joyful, fulfilling life you envision. Writing down your goals and tracking your progress will help bring these principles to life and keep you moving forward with energy and focus.

Let's dive into the power of action as a catalyst for growth and joyful living!

ACTION

The Energy and Power That Keeps You Moving Along the Path of Joyful Living

> "Take the first step in faith. You don't have to see the whole staircase, just take the first step.
> —Marin Luther King, Jr.

SUMMARY:

Chapter 6 explores the transformative power of action, emphasizing how consistent, intentional steps bring you closer to your goals and dreams. Through the power word

"Action," you're invited to shift from passive observation to active participation, taking charge of your life's direction. Progress isn't about massive leaps but is achieved through small, steady efforts that build momentum over time.

In this chapter, you'll discover the 4 Cs—Commitment, Courage, Capability, and Confidence—as pillars that support each step you take toward meaningful progress. Embracing the discomfort that comes with growth becomes a valuable part of your journey, reminding you that you're stretching, learning, and moving forward. Through the power of action, you'll begin to create positive change and pursue your dreams with determination and resilience, filling your life with purpose and joy.

Putting on the power of action means choosing to live fully engaged, knowing that each step forward is bringing you closer to the life you truly desire.

QUESTIONS FOR REFLECTION:

1. **Overcoming Fear and Uncertainty**. Reflect on a time when fear or uncertainty held you back from taking action. What specific thoughts or beliefs created this hesitation, and how did you eventually find the courage to move forward? How might recognizing these patterns empower you to take more decisive action in the future?

2. **Commitment as a Catalyst**. Consider the power of commitment as a motivator for action. How does making a promise to yourself create accountability and inspire you to pursue your goals with focus and persistence? In what areas of your life could a deeper commitment bring you closer to your aspirations?

3. **Building Capability Through Consistency**. Think about the link between capability and consistent action. How does taking intentional steps, even small ones, help you build the skills, knowledge, and confidence needed to reach your goals? How might celebrating each step enhance your sense of progress?

4. **The Role of Courage in Growth**. Reflect on the importance of courage in taking action. How does embracing discomfort and pushing past fear contribute to your personal and professional growth? How can courage help you face new challenges with resilience and optimism?

5. **Creating Determination and Confidence**. Identify the thoughts or beliefs you need to foster a sense of determination, commitment, and confidence. What would you need to focus on to feel certain about the outcomes you want to create? How might these empowering thoughts shape your actions and bring you closer to success?

WORD POWER ACTIVITY:

1. **Reframe Discomfort as Growth**. Challenge yourself to step outside your comfort zone by trying a new activity or pursuing a goal that stretches you. As feelings of discomfort arise, approach them with curiosity instead of resistance, seeing them as signs of growth and progress. Embrace this mindset as a powerful step forward.

2. **Reflect on Past Successes**. Take time to remember past moments where you took action and succeeded, no matter how big or small. Celebrate the lessons you learned and the persistence that led you to these achievements. Let this reflection remind you of the incredible power of consistent effort and determination in creating meaningful change.

CHAPTER 7:

To fully embrace the ideas in Chapter 7, *Appreciate*, I suggest reading this chapter in *The Word Effect: 7 Simple Words to Create Your Most Beautiful Life* or watching the corresponding segment in *The Word Effect* video course. In this chapter, we explore how the power of appreciation transforms not just our mindset but also our experiences, helping us savor the beauty and wonder that life offers.

Appreciation invites us to pause, reflect, and truly enjoy the present, bringing a new sense of joy and contentment into our daily lives. As you read or watch, consider the moments, people, and experiences you can appreciate today. Keep a journal close by to capture these reflections—when you document what you're grateful for, you build a mindset that celebrates abundance and lets you find joy in the journey, not just in reaching the destination.

APPRECIATE

The Power Word That Lets You Enjoy the Beauty and Wonder of the Journey

"Appreciation can make a day, even change a life. Your willingness to put it into words is all that is necessary."
—Margaret Cousins

SUMMARY:

In Chapter 7, we dive into the transformative power of *Appreciate*, a word that invites us to see and savor the richness and beauty woven into every day. By embracing appreciation, we learn to value our experiences, relationships, and surroundings with fresh eyes, recognizing their unique beauty and worth. Shifting our focus to gratitude for the present moment allows us to cultivate greater joy, curiosity, and fulfillment.

Through personal stories and inspiring insights, this chapter shows how appreciation can open doors to deeper connections and personal growth. It's about choosing to celebrate life's blessings, leaning into curiosity rather than fear, and making deliberate choices that honor what truly matters. As you explore this chapter, you're encouraged to harness the power of *Appreciate* to nurture joy and prioritize the things that fill your life with meaning.

QUESTIONS FOR REFLECTION:

1. **Transforming Through Appreciation**. Reflect on a time when appreciation transformed your outlook or mindset. How did recognizing the value and beauty in a particular experience or relationship impact your sense of joy and fulfillment?

2. **What Matters Most**. Consider the concept of appreciating what truly matters. How does recognizing the inherent value of your experiences, relationships, and surroundings foster a sense of fulfillment and contentment?

3. **Living in the Present**. Explore how shifting your focus to the present moment can enhance your ability to appreciate life's blessings. How might this perspective bring greater joy and fulfillment into your daily life?

4. **Finding Joy in Simplicity**. Reflect on the idea that less can often be more, especially when it comes to time management. How can embracing simplicity, self-care, and rest contribute to a deeper sense of balance and well-being?

5. **Creating Space for Joy**. How can prioritizing appreciation over the rush of daily demands help you create space for joy, meaningful connections, and personal growth? Consider what intentional choices you might make to live more fully in gratitude.

Let each reflection guide you toward embracing appreciation as a powerful tool for a more joyful and intentional life.

WORD POWER ACTIVITY:

1. **Gratitude Notebook**. Start a daily gratitude or appreciation notebook, where you jot down five things you're grateful for or that you appreciate each day. Reflect on the positive experiences, relationships, and blessings in your life, no matter how small, and notice how this habit begins to lift your outlook.

2. **Appreciate the Little Things**. Practice redirecting your mind to notice and appreciate the little things. Take a mindful walk or engage in a daily appreciation exercise, noticing the beauty around you, the kindness of others, or the simple joys of everyday life. Allow this practice to cultivate wonder and gratitude in the present.

3. **Embrace Simplicity and Self-Care**. Embrace simplicity by prioritizing self-care, rest, and enjoyment in your daily life. Give yourself permission to slow down, say no to unnecessary commitments, and focus on activities that genuinely nourish your body, mind, and spirit. Notice how embracing simplicity enhances your sense of fulfillment and balance.

Use these activities to foster an appreciation-filled life, one where each day holds space for gratitude, balance, and a more intentional focus on what truly matters.

CHAPTER 8:

In this chapter of *The Word Effect: 7 Simple Words to Create Your Most Beautiful Life*, we explore the transformative power of "Aspire." Begin by reading Chapter 8 in the book or watching the video for this chapter in *The Word Effect* course. Aspire is a word that invites us to lift our vision, stretch our creativity, and imagine the possibilities that lie ahead. By focusing on our aspirations, we open doors to new ideas, fuel our motivation, and create a clearer path toward our dreams.

As you move through this chapter, consider how aspiring to new heights can enrich your life. Keep a journal close by to capture your reflections and the ideas that arise. Writing helps make your aspirations tangible, giving you a starting point for taking purposeful action. This chapter is an invitation to see beyond the limits of today and embrace a mindset of possibility, where creativity and imagination shape a more beautiful life.

ASPIRE

The Power Word That Inspires Creativity and Imagination

"Becoming the person you aspire to requires that you stop
being that old self."
—Joe Dispenza

SUMMARY:

Chapter 8 explores the empowering essence of the word "Aspire," encouraging us to ignite our creativity, imagination, and potential for personal growth. To aspire is to focus our hopes and ambitions on meaningful pursuits, embracing a journey of self-discovery as we move closer to our highest potential. In this chapter, I invite you to cultivate presence in the moment, recognizing the inherent worth and progress you embody right now—without waiting for perfection. Aspire isn't about an endpoint; it's about the ongoing journey of becoming, where each step forward brings new insights, creativity, and possibilities.

As you read, consider how you can trust the process of aspiration, celebrate your achievements, and approach each day with a mindset of abundance and hope. This chapter calls on you to dream, reach, and imagine a life aligned with your deepest desires. With the power of "Aspire," you can create a life that reflects the beauty and joy of your unique path, embracing each day as an opportunity to move closer to the person you are meant to be.

QUESTIONS FOR REFLECTION:

1. **Embracing Aspiration.** Reflect on a time when you felt inspired to pursue a goal or dream. What emotions and thoughts accompanied this feeling, and how did it impact your actions? How can you rekindle that sense of aspiration in your current life?

2. **Visualizing Potential.** Consider the phrase "highest potential." What does reaching your highest potential look like to you? How might embracing your creativity and imagination help you move closer to this vision?

3. **Presence and Progress.** How does practicing presence—focusing on where you are today—help you recognize your progress? In what ways can you celebrate your journey, even if you're not yet where you ultimately want to be?

4. **Abundance Mindset.** Reflect on the concept of abundance in relation to your goals and dreams. How can you shift your mindset to see opportunities rather than limitations? How might this perspective open up new possibilities for personal and professional growth?

5. **Trusting the Process.** Think about a current aspiration or project. How can trusting the process of gradual progress help you let go of perfectionism and move forward? What small, intentional steps can you take this week to bring you closer to your aspirations?

WORD POWER ACTIVITY:

1. **Create a Vision Board of Aspirations.** Spend some time gathering images, words, and symbols that represent your dreams, goals, and aspirations. Arrange them on a vision board to serve as a daily reminder of where you want to go. Reflect on this vision board regularly to stay inspired and focused on the steps that can help you reach your highest potential.

2. **Daily "Aspire" Affirmation Practice.** Choose an affirmation that resonates with your aspirations, such as "I am moving closer to my highest potential every day" or "I embrace creativity and possibility." Write it down and place it somewhere visible. Repeat it each morning to set a positive, inspired tone for your day, reminding yourself of your potential to grow and achieve.

CONCLUSION:

To complete your journey through *The Word Effect: 7 Simple Words to Create Your Most Beautiful Life*, I invite you to revisit this final chapter in the book or watch the concluding video in *The Word Effect* course. In this conclusion, we reflect on the power of words as a continuous cycle—a way to lead your life intentionally, with joy and purpose. Each word in this journey, from "Acknowledge" to "Aspire," serves as a guide to help you navigate challenges and celebrate growth.

By embracing *The Word Effect*, you empower yourself to live a joyful life in every season. Remember, joyful living is a journey, not a destination, and these words are your compass to help you find meaning and beauty along the way.

THE WORD EFFECT'S NEVER-ENDING CYCLE OF JOYFUL LIVING

"The joy we feel has little to do with the circumstances of our lives and everything to do with the focus of our lives."
—Russell M. Nelson

SUMMARY:

As you complete this journey through *The Word Effect: 7 Simple Words to Create Your Most Beautiful Life*, reflect on how each of these seven words—Acknowledge, Ask, Accept, Abundance, Action, Appreciate, and Aspire—guides you toward a life filled with joy, purpose, and intention. This isn't just a one-time shift; it's a continuous, empowering cycle that helps you return to what matters most. These words act like a compass, gently directing you back to your core values and aspirations, even when life feels uncertain or doesn't go as planned.

Living joyfully is not about achieving perfection but about intentionally choosing words that create a fulfilling, beautiful life. Through *The Word Effect*, you have the power to transform challenges into growth, scarcity into abundance, and fear into courage. Each day, as you choose to put on these words, remember they are your tools to build a life of resilience, gratitude, and inner peace. Let them help you lead from within and trust in your potential to create your most beautiful life—one intentional word at a time.

So, as you step forward, let these words shape your thoughts, actions, and reality. Embrace the power they bring and carry them with you as lifelong companions on your path of joyful, purposeful living. Here's to living each day with intention, gratitude, and a renewed spirit of aspiration. The journey continues, and it's yours to create.

QUESTIONS FOR REFLECTION:

1. **Inspired Change**. Reflect on a time when you felt inspired to make a meaningful change in your life. How did shifting your focus and language influence your perspective and actions? What insights did you gain from this experience?
2. **Perseverance and Trust in Joyful Living**. Consider the importance of perseverance and trust in the journey toward joyful living. How can committing to consistent effort and believing in the power of words help you overcome obstacles and setbacks along the way?
3. **Intentionality and Joy**. Think about the role of intentionality in creating a joyful life. How can consciously choosing and practicing words that align with your values and aspirations empower you to shape the reality you desire?
4. **Discovering Your Own Word Effect**. Explore the idea of discovering your personal Word Effect. How can embracing the transformative power of words and the cycle outlined in *The Word Effect: 7 Simple Words to Create Your Most Beautiful Life* empower you to create your most beautiful life?
5. **Intentional Leadership and Speaking Success**. As a leader, how can intentional language help you cultivate creativity and innovation within yourself and your

team? How will you "speak your success" to inspire those around you and foster a culture of growth?

WORD POWER ACTIVITY:

1. **Practice the Word Effect Cycle**. Integrate the Word Effect's cycle into your daily life by choosing words that resonate with your goals, values, and aspirations. Begin by acknowledging where you are, ask for guidance when needed, accept yourself unconditionally, focus on abundance, take empowered action, appreciate the good, and look up as you aspire toward your highest potential. Notice how each word guides you to a mindset of growth and possibility.

2. **Engage with a Supportive Community**. Seek connection with a community or mentor who can provide encouragement, guidance, and accountability as you pursue joyful living. Surrounding yourself with people who uplift and inspire you will reinforce the power of words and help you create your most beautiful life. Let their support remind you of the positive impact words can have on your journey.

INVITATION TO SHARE:

As you embark on your journey to discover your own Word Effect, I invite you to extend this experience by sharing it with others. By embracing intentional language in your life, you'll naturally become a beacon of positivity and influence for those around you. Your words, insights, and personal growth can inspire and uplift others on their own paths toward joyful living. Let words be your compass, guiding you and those you reach toward a life filled with purpose and intention.

Your voice truly has the power to make a difference. Together, let's create a ripple effect of positivity, empowerment, and transformation—one word at a time.

www.becomingwithbecky.com

ABOUT THE AUTHOR

Driven by the desire to spread and inspire goodness, Becky Kemp is dedicated to sharing the power found in positive words. From the onset of her clothing brand, Becoming Threads, to her current podcast, called "The Word Effect," she loves speaking and coaching about how words matter!

Becky is a certified life coach and mentor who is dedicated to helping others recognize that change is possible and that each of us is capable of creating a beautiful life. She also serves as a board member of the National Speaker's Association, Mountain West Chapter and in the National Speakers Association, and is an active volunteer in her church and community.

Becky is married to her high school sweetheart and the mother of five children. In her free time, she loves quiet early mornings; walking her dog, Marley; boating on Lake Powell with her family; and watching her son still at home play baseball.

For more information on Becky's coaching services and women's retreats or to book her to speak at your next function, visit www.becomingwithbecky.com. Follow Becky on Facebook and Instagram @becomingwithbecky and subscribe to "The Word Effect" podcast on your favorite app to listen to podcasts.